The Success Journal

BY HOOKED LIVING

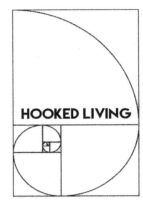

HOOKED LIVING

LIVE BY CHOICE, NOT BY CHANCE
™

Hooked Living Journals
Created to Guide People to awaken and live
from their heart

Thank you

Find more information about Hooked Living at:

Website - www.hookedliving.co.uk   Instagram - @hookedliving

Cover and Journal design by Miker Hook

ISBN: 9798740356358   **Imprint:** Independently published

The Success Journal

BY HOOKED LIVING

This Journal Belongs to:

I choose to be
the predominant creative force in my life
and
live life in my highest vibration

Rules for being Human

FROM ANCIENT SANSKRIT

- YOU WILL RECEIVE A BODY

- YOU WILL LEARN LESSONS

- THERE ARE NO MISTAKES, ONLY LESSONS

- A LESSON WILL BE REPEATED UNTIL IT IS LEARNED

- LEARNING LESSONS DOES NOT END

- 'THERE' IS NOT BETTER THAN 'HERE'

- OTHERS ARE MERELY MIRRORS OF YOU

- WHAT YOU MAKE OF YOUR LIFE IS UP TO YOU

- LIFE IS EXACTLY WHAT YOU THINK IT IS

- YOUR ANSWERS LIE INSIDE OF YOU

- YOU WILL FORGET ALL OF THIS

- YOU CAN REMEMBER IT WHENEVER YOU WANT

Every day we get the chance to start again.

It's all up to you...

Achieving My Goals

THE SIMPLE METHOD TO SUCCESS

★ Write 10 Goals you would like to achieve in the next 12 months
Write the goals in the present tense in the **'My 10 Goals'** page...

Example:
I earn...
I live...
I achieve...
I create powerful journals to guide people to create their dreams...

Whatever it is you want to create...
You may already have a set of ***End Results*** you want to achieve, if so write these down in the **'My 10 Goals'** page.

★ Now say:

'If I could have any one goal on my list within 24 hours, which one goal would have the greatest positive impact on my life?'

This will usually jump out at you...

★ Put a circle around that goal,
and do only specific tasks for that goal until it's complete

★ That's the goal you transfer to the **'Creating my Goal'** page and then follow the '7 steps'

Follow your bliss and the Universe will open doors for you where there were only walls.

– Joseph Campbell

My 10 Goals

TODAY'S DATE:_____

1. _____
2. _____
3. _____
4. _____
5. _____
6. _____
7. _____
8. _____
9. _____
10. _____

Whatever the mind can conceive and believe, it can achieve

- Napoleon Hill

7 steps to Creating my Goal

THE SIMPLE METHOD TO SUCCESS

1. The Goal I am creating:

_____

_____

2. I will achieve my goal by... (add a Date):

_____

3. The things I am doing to achieve my goal:

_____

_____

_____

_____

_____

_____

_____

The best way to predict the future is to Create it....

- Abraham Lincoln

7 steps to Creating my Goal

THE SIMPLE METHOD TO SUCCESS

4. Organise the steps into a check list:

- [ ]
- [ ]
- [ ]
- [ ]
- [ ]
- [ ]
- [ ]
- [ ]
- [ ]

5. Set the Intention to **_Take action_** towards it.

6. **_Every day_** write the goal, write the action and take the action towards **_The Goal_**.

7. When you achieve it, go to the list of Goals and choose the next Goal in the same way as before.

If you follow this simple method you can achieve anything!

Nothing can stop you but yourself...

Hooked Living

Notes

ANYTHING ELSE YOU WOULD LIKE TO ADD

Let's Create

TODAY'S DATE:

DAILY GRATITUDE	TASKS FOR THE DAY
★	☐
★	☐
★	☐
★	☐
★	☐
★	☐

TODAY'S ACTION STEP TOWARDS MY GOAL

GOAL:

Daily Notes

Let's Create

TODAY'S DATE:

DAILY GRATITUDE

★ ....

★ ....

★ ....

★ ....

★ ....

★ ....

TASKS FOR THE DAY

☐ ....

☐ ....

☐ ....

☐ ....

☐ ....

☐ ....

TODAY'S ACTION STEP TOWARDS MY GOAL

GOAL:

Daily Notes

Let's Create

TODAY'S DATE:

DAILY GRATITUDE

★ ....

★ ....

★ ....

★ ....

★ ....

★ ....

TASKS FOR THE DAY

☐ ....

☐ ....

☐ ....

☐ ....

☐ ....

☐ ....

TODAY'S ACTION STEP TOWARDS MY GOAL

GOAL:

_____

_____

_____

_____

_____

Daily Notes

Let's Create

TODAY'S DATE:

DAILY GRATITUDE

★ ....

★ ....

★ ....

★ ....

★ ....

★ ....

TASKS FOR THE DAY

☐

☐

☐

☐

☐

☐

TODAY'S ACTION STEP TOWARDS MY GOAL

GOAL:

_____

_____

_____

_____

Daily Notes

Let's Create

TODAY'S DATE:

DAILY GRATITUDE

★ ....

★ ....

★ ....

★ ....

★ ....

★ ....

TASKS FOR THE DAY

☐ ....

☐ ....

☐ ....

☐ ....

☐ ....

☐ ....

TODAY'S ACTION STEP TOWARDS MY GOAL

GOAL:

_____

_____

_____

_____

_____

Daily Notes

Let's Create

TODAY'S DATE:

DAILY GRATITUDE	TASKS FOR THE DAY

⭐ ....

☐ ....

⭐ ....

☐ ....

⭐ ....

☐ ....

⭐ ....

☐ ....

⭐ ....

☐ ....

⭐ ....

☐ ....

TODAY'S ACTION STEP TOWARDS MY GOAL

GOAL:

Daily Notes

Let's Create

TODAY'S DATE:

DAILY GRATITUDE

★ ....

★ ....

★ ....

★ ....

★ ....

★ ....

TASKS FOR THE DAY

☐ ....

☐ ....

☐ ....

☐ ....

☐ ....

☐ ....

TODAY'S ACTION STEP TOWARDS MY GOAL

GOAL:

_____

_____

_____

_____

Daily Notes

Let's Create

TODAY'S DATE:

DAILY GRATITUDE

★ ....

★ ....

★ ....

★ ....

★ ....

★ ....

TASKS FOR THE DAY

☐ ....

☐ ....

☐ ....

☐ ....

☐ ....

☐ ....

TODAY'S ACTION STEP TOWARDS MY GOAL

GOAL:

_____

_____

_____

_____

Daily Notes

Let's Create

TODAY'S DATE:

DAILY GRATITUDE	TASKS FOR THE DAY
⭐	☐ ....
⭐	☐ ....
⭐	☐ ....
⭐	☐ ....
⭐	☐ ....
⭐	☐ ....

TODAY'S ACTION STEP TOWARDS MY GOAL

GOAL:

_____

_____

_____

_____

Daily Notes

Let's Create

TODAY'S DATE:

DAILY GRATITUDE

TASKS FOR THE DAY

★ .... ☐ ....

★ .... ☐ ....

★ .... ☐ ....

★ .... ☐ ....

★ .... ☐ ....

★ .... ☐ ....

TODAY'S ACTION STEP TOWARDS MY GOAL

GOAL:

_____

_____

_____

_____

_____

Daily Notes

Let's Create

TODAY'S DATE:

DAILY GRATITUDE

★ ....

★ ....

★ ....

★ ....

★ ....

★ ....

TASKS FOR THE DAY

☐ ....

☐ ....

☐ ....

☐ ....

☐ ....

☐ ....

TODAY'S ACTION STEP TOWARDS MY GOAL

GOAL:

_____

_____

_____

_____

Daily Notes

Let's Create

TODAY'S DATE:

DAILY GRATITUDE

★ ....

★ ....

★ ....

★ ....

★ ....

★ ....

TASKS FOR THE DAY

☐ ....

☐ ....

☐ ....

☐ ....

☐ ....

☐ ....

TODAY'S ACTION STEP TOWARDS MY GOAL

GOAL:

_____

_____

_____

_____

_____

Daily Notes

Let's Create

TODAY'S DATE:

DAILY GRATITUDE	TASKS FOR THE DAY

★ .... ☐ ....

★ .... ☐ ....

★ .... ☐ ....

★ .... ☐ ....

★ .... ☐ ....

★ .... ☐ ....

TODAY'S ACTION STEP TOWARDS MY GOAL

GOAL:

_____

_____

_____

_____

Daily Notes

Let's Create

TODAY'S DATE:

DAILY GRATITUDE

★ ....

★ ....

★ ....

★ ....

★ ....

★ ....

TASKS FOR THE DAY

☐ ....

☐ ....

☐ ....

☐ ....

☐ ....

☐ ....

TODAY'S ACTION STEP TOWARDS MY GOAL

GOAL:

_____

_____

_____

_____

_____

Daily Notes

Let's Create

TODAY'S DATE:

DAILY GRATITUDE

⭐ ....

⭐ ....

⭐ ....

⭐ ....

⭐ ....

⭐ ....

TASKS FOR THE DAY

☐ ....

☐ ....

☐ ....

☐ ....

☐ ....

☐ ....

TODAY'S ACTION STEP TOWARDS MY GOAL

GOAL:

Daily Notes

Let's Create

TODAY'S DATE:

DAILY GRATITUDE

★ ....
★ ....
★ ....
★ ....
★ ....
★ ....

TASKS FOR THE DAY

☐ ....
☐ ....
☐ ....
☐ ....
☐ ....
☐ ....

TODAY'S ACTION STEP TOWARDS MY GOAL

GOAL:

_____

_____

_____

_____

Daily Notes

Let's Create

TODAY'S DATE:

DAILY GRATITUDE

★ ....

★ ....

★ ....

★ ....

★ ....

★ ....

TASKS FOR THE DAY

☐ ....

☐ ....

☐ ....

☐ ....

☐ ....

☐ ....

TODAY'S ACTION STEP TOWARDS MY GOAL

GOAL:

Daily Notes

Let's Create

TODON'S DATE:

DAILY GRATITUDE

★ ....
★ ....
★ ....
★ ....
★ ....
★ ....

TASKS FOR THE DAY

☐ ....
☐ ....
☐ ....
☐ ....
☐ ....
☐ ....

TODAY'S ACTION STEP TOWARDS MY GOAL

GOAL:

_____

_____

_____

_____

Daily Notes

Let's Create

TODAY'S DATE:

DAILY GRATITUDE

TASKS FOR THE DAY

★ ....

☐ ....

★ ....

☐ ....

★ ....

☐ ....

★ ....

☐ ....

★ ....

☐ ....

★ ....

☐ ....

TODAY'S ACTION STEP TOWARDS MY GOAL

GOAL:

Daily Notes

Let's Create

TODAY'S DATE:

DAILY GRATITUDE

★ ....

★ ....

★ ....

★ ....

★ ....

★ ....

TASKS FOR THE DAY

☐ ....

☐ ....

☐ ....

☐ ....

☐ ....

☐ ....

TODAY'S ACTION STEP TOWARDS MY GOAL

GOAL:

_____

_____

_____

_____

Daily Notes

Let's Create

TODAY'S DATE:

DAILY GRATITUDE

TASKS FOR THE DAY

⭐ ....

☐ ....

⭐ ....

☐ ....

⭐ ....

☐ ....

⭐ ....

☐ ....

⭐ ....

☐ ....

⭐ ....

☐ ....

TODAY'S ACTION STEP TOWARDS MY GOAL

GOAL:

Daily Notes

Let's Create

TODODAY'S DATE:

DAILY GRATITUDE

★ ....

★ ....

★ ....

★ ....

★ ....

★ ....

TASKS FOR THE DAY

☐ ....

☐ ....

☐ ....

☐ ....

☐ ....

☐ ....

TODAY'S ACTION STEP TOWARDS MY GOAL

GOAL:

Daily Notes

Let's Create

TODAY'S DATE:

DAILY GRATITUDE

★ ....

★ ....

★ ....

★ ....

★ ....

★ ....

TASKS FOR THE DAY

☐ ....

☐ ....

☐ ....

☐ ....

☐ ....

☐ ....

TODAY'S ACTION STEP TOWARDS MY GOAL

GOAL:

_____

_____

_____

_____

_____

Daily Notes

Let's Create

TODAY'S DATE:

DAILY GRATITUDE

★ ....

★ ....

★ ....

★ ....

★ ....

★ ....

TASKS FOR THE DAY

☐ ....

☐ ....

☐ ....

☐ ....

☐ ....

☐ ....

TODAY'S ACTION STEP TOWARDS MY GOAL

GOAL:

Daily Notes

Let's Create

TODAY'S DATE:

DAILY GRATITUDE

★ ....

★ ....

★ ....

★ ....

★ ....

★ ....

TASKS FOR THE DAY

☐ ....

☐ ....

☐ ....

☐ ....

☐ ....

☐ ....

TODAY'S ACTION STEP TOWARDS MY GOAL

GOAL:

_____

_____

_____

_____

Daily Notes

Let's Create

TODAY'S DATE:

DAILY GRATITUDE

★ ....

★ ....

★ ....

★ ....

★ ....

★ ....

TASKS FOR THE DAY

☐ ....

☐ ....

☐ ....

☐ ....

☐ ....

☐ ....

TODAY'S ACTION STEP TOWARDS MY GOAL

GOAL:

_____

_____

_____

_____

_____

Daily Notes

Let's Create

TODAY'S DATE:

DAILY GRATITUDE	TASKS FOR THE DAY

★ .... ☐ ....

★ .... ☐ ....

★ .... ☐ ....

★ .... ☐ ....

★ .... ☐ ....

★ .... ☐ ....

TODAY'S ACTION STEP TOWARDS MY GOAL

GOAL:

_____

_____

_____

_____

_____

Daily Notes

Let's Create

TODAY'S DATE:

DAILY GRATITUDE

★ ....

★ ....

★ ....

★ ....

★ ....

★ ....

TASKS FOR THE DAY

☐

☐

☐

☐

☐

☐

TODAY'S ACTION STEP TOWARDS MY GOAL

GOAL:

Daily Notes

Let's Create

TODAY'S DATE:

DAILY GRATITUDE

★

★

★

★

★

★

TASKS FOR THE DAY

☐

☐

☐

☐

☐

☐

TODAY'S ACTION STEP TOWARDS MY GOAL

GOAL:

Daily Notes

Let's Create

TODAY'S DATE:

DAILY GRATITUDE

★ ....
★ ....
★ ....
★ ....
★ ....
★ ....

TASKS FOR THE DAY

☐ ....
☐ ....
☐ ....
☐ ....
☐ ....
☐ ....

TODAY'S ACTION STEP TOWARDS MY GOAL

GOAL:

_____

_____

_____

_____

_____

Daily Notes

Let's Create

TODAY'S DATE:

DAILY GRATITUDE	TASKS FOR THE DAY

★ .... ☐ ....

★ .... ☐ ....

★ .... ☐ ....

★ .... ☐ ....

★ .... ☐ ....

★ .... ☐ ....

TODAY'S ACTION STEP TOWARDS MY GOAL

GOAL:

_____

_____

_____

_____

_____

Daily Notes

Let's Create

TODAY'S DATE:

DAILY GRATITUDE

★ ....

★ ....

★ ....

★ ....

★ ....

★ ....

TASKS FOR THE DAY

☐

☐

☐

☐

☐

☐

TODAY'S ACTION STEP TOWARDS MY GOAL

GOAL:

_____

_____

_____

_____

_____

Daily Notes

Let's Create

TODAY'S DATE:

DAILY GRATITUDE

★ ....

★ ....

★ ....

★ ....

★ ....

★ ....

TASKS FOR THE DAY

☐ ....

☐ ....

☐ ....

☐ ....

☐ ....

☐ ....

TODAY'S ACTION STEP TOWARDS MY GOAL

GOAL:

Daily Notes

Let's Create

TODAY'S DATE:

DAILY GRATITUDE

TASKS FOR THE DAY

⭐ ....

☐ ....

⭐ ....

☐ ....

⭐ ....

☐ ....

⭐ ....

☐ ....

⭐ ....

☐ ....

⭐ ....

☐ ....

TODAY'S ACTION STEP TOWARDS MY GOAL

GOAL:

Daily Notes

Let's Create

TODAY'S DATE:

DAILY GRATITUDE

★
★
★
★
★
★

TASKS FOR THE DAY

☐
☐
☐
☐
☐
☐

TODAY'S ACTION STEP TOWARDS MY GOAL

GOAL:

Daily Notes

Let's Create

TODAY'S DATE:

DAILY GRATITUDE	TASKS FOR THE DAY
★	☐
★	☐
★	☐
★	☐
★	☐
★	☐

TODAY'S ACTION STEP TOWARDS MY GOAL

GOAL:

Daily Notes

Let's Create

TODAY'S DATE:

DAILY GRATITUDE

★ ....
★ ....
★ ....
★ ....
★ ....
★ ....

TASKS FOR THE DAY

☐ ....
☐ ....
☐ ....
☐ ....
☐ ....
☐ ....

TODAY'S ACTION STEP TOWARDS MY GOAL

GOAL:

Daily Notes

Let's Create

DAILY GRATITUDE	TASKS FOR THE DAY
★	☐
★	☐
★	☐
★	☐
★	☐
★	☐

TODAY'S ACTION STEP TOWARDS MY GOAL

GOAL:

Daily Notes

Let's Create

TODAY'S DATE:

DAILY GRATITUDE	TASKS FOR THE DAY
★	☐ ....
★	☐ ....
★	☐ ....
★	☐ ....
★	☐ ....
★	☐ ....

TODAY'S ACTION STEP TOWARDS MY GOAL

GOAL:

_____

_____

_____

_____

_____

Daily Notes

Let's Create

TODAY'S DATE:

DAILY GRATITUDE	TASKS FOR THE DAY
★	☐
★	☐
★	☐
★	☐
★	☐
★	☐

TODAY'S ACTION STEP TOWARDS MY GOAL

GOAL:

Daily Notes

Let's Create

TODAY'S DATE:

DAILY GRATITUDE	TASKS FOR THE DAY

★ .... ☐ ....

★ .... ☐ ....

★ .... ☐ ....

★ .... ☐ ....

★ .... ☐ ....

★ .... ☐ ....

TODAY'S ACTION STEP TOWARDS MY GOAL

GOAL:

_____

_____

_____

_____

Daily Notes

Let's Create

TODAY'S DATE:

DAILY GRATITUDE

TASKS FOR THE DAY

★ .... ☐ ....

★ .... ☐ ....

★ .... ☐ ....

★ .... ☐ ....

★ .... ☐ ....

★ .... ☐ ....

TODAY'S ACTION STEP TOWARDS MY GOAL

GOAL:

Daily Notes

Let's Create

TODAY'S DATE:

DAILY GRATITUDE

★ ....

★ ....

★ ....

★ ....

★ ....

★ ....

TASKS FOR THE DAY

☐ ....

☐ ....

☐ ....

☐ ....

☐ ....

☐ ....

TODAY'S ACTION STEP TOWARDS MY GOAL

GOAL:

_____

_____

_____

_____

_____

Daily Notes

Let's Create

TODAY'S DATE:

DAILY GRATITUDE

★ ....

★ ....

★ ....

★ ....

★ ....

★ ....

TASKS FOR THE DAY

☐ ....

☐ ....

☐ ....

☐ ....

☐ ....

☐ ....

TODAY'S ACTION STEP TOWARDS MY GOAL

GOAL:

_____

_____

_____

_____

_____

Daily Notes

Let's Create

TODAY'S DATE:

DAILY GRATITUDE

★ ....

★ ....

★ ....

★ ....

★ ....

★ ....

TASKS FOR THE DAY

☐ ....

☐ ....

☐ ....

☐ ....

☐ ....

☐ ....

TODAY'S ACTION STEP TOWARDS MY GOAL

GOAL:

_____

_____

_____

_____

_____

Daily Notes

Let's Create

TODAY'S DATE:

DAILY GRATITUDE

★ ....

★ ....

★ ....

★ ....

★ ....

★ ....

TASKS FOR THE DAY

☐ ....

☐ ....

☐ ....

☐ ....

☐ ....

☐ ....

TODAY'S ACTION STEP TOWARDS MY GOAL

GOAL:

Daily Notes

Let's Create

TODAY'S DATE:

DAILY GRATITUDE	TASKS FOR THE DAY
⭐	☐
⭐	☐
⭐	☐
⭐	☐
⭐	☐
⭐	☐

TODAY'S ACTION STEP TOWARDS MY GOAL

GOAL:

Daily Notes

Let's Create

TODAY'S DATE:

DAILY GRATITUDE	TASKS FOR THE DAY
★	☐ ....
★	☐ ....
★	☐ ....
★	☐ ....
★	☐ ....
★	☐ ....

TODAY'S ACTION STEP TOWARDS MY GOAL

GOAL:

_____

_____

_____

_____

Daily Notes

Let's Create

TODAY'S DATE:

DAILY GRATITUDE

⭐ ....

⭐ ....

⭐ ....

⭐ ....

⭐ ....

⭐ ....

TASKS FOR THE DAY

☐ _____

☐ _____

☐ _____

☐ _____

☐ _____

☐ _____

TODAY'S ACTION STEP TOWARDS MY GOAL

GOAL:

_____

_____

_____

_____

_____

Daily Notes

Let's Create

TODAY'S DATE:

DAILY GRATITUDE

★ ....

★ ....

★ ....

★ ....

★ ....

★ ....

TASKS FOR THE DAY

☐ ....

☐ ....

☐ ....

☐ ....

☐ ....

☐ ....

TODAY'S ACTION STEP TOWARDS MY GOAL

GOAL:

Daily Notes

Let's Create

TODAY'S DATE:

DAILY GRATITUDE

⭐ ....

⭐ ....

⭐ ....

⭐ ....

⭐ ....

⭐ ....

TASKS FOR THE DAY

☐ ....

☐ ....

☐ ....

☐ ....

☐ ....

☐ ....

TODAY'S ACTION STEP TOWARDS MY GOAL

GOAL:

_____

_____

_____

_____

_____

Daily Notes

Let's Create

TODAY'S DATE:

DAILY GRATITUDE

TASKS FOR THE DAY

★ .... ☐ ....

★ .... ☐ ....

★ .... ☐ ....

★ .... ☐ ....

★ .... ☐ ....

★ .... ☐ ....

TODAY'S ACTION STEP TOWARDS MY GOAL

GOAL:

Daily Notes

Let's Create

TODAY'S DATE:

DAILY GRATITUDE

★ ....

★ ....

★ ....

★ ....

★ ....

★ ....

TASKS FOR THE DAY

☐

☐

☐

☐

☐

☐

TODAY'S ACTION STEP TOWARDS MY GOAL

GOAL:

Daily Notes

Let's Create

TODAY'S DATE:

DAILY GRATITUDE

TASKS FOR THE DAY

★ .... ☐ ....

★ .... ☐ ....

★ .... ☐ ....

★ .... ☐ ....

★ .... ☐ ....

★ .... ☐ ....

TODAY'S ACTION STEP TOWARDS MY GOAL

GOAL:

Daily Notes

Let's Create

TODAY'S DATE:

DAILY GRATITUDE

★ ....

★ ....

★ ....

★ ....

★ ....

★ ....

TASKS FOR THE DAY

☐ ....

☐ ....

☐ ....

☐ ....

☐ ....

☐ ....

TODAY'S ACTION STEP TOWARDS MY GOAL

GOAL:

_____

_____

_____

_____

_____

Daily Notes

Let's Create

TODAY'S DATE:

DAILY GRATITUDE

★ ....

★ ....

★ ....

★ ....

★ ....

★ ....

TASKS FOR THE DAY

☐ ....

☐ ....

☐ ....

☐ ....

☐ ....

☐ ....

TODAY'S ACTION STEP TOWARDS MY GOAL

GOAL:

_____

_____

_____

_____

_____

Daily Notes

Let's Create

TODAY'S DATE:

DAILY GRATITUDE

★ ....

★ ....

★ ....

★ ....

★ ....

★ ....

TASKS FOR THE DAY

☐ ....

☐ ....

☐ ....

☐ ....

☐ ....

☐ ....

TODAY'S ACTION STEP TOWARDS MY GOAL

GOAL:

Daily Notes

Let's Create

TODAY'S DATE:

DAILY GRATITUDE	TASKS FOR THE DAY
★	☐
★	☐
★	☐
★	☐
★	☐
★	☐

TODAY'S ACTION STEP TOWARDS MY GOAL

GOAL:

Daily Notes

Let's Create

TODAY'S DATE:

DAILY GRATITUDE

★ ....

★ ....

★ ....

★ ....

★ ....

★ ....

TASKS FOR THE DAY

☐ ....

☐ ....

☐ ....

☐ ....

☐ ....

☐ ....

TODAY'S ACTION STEP TOWARDS MY GOAL

GOAL:

_____

_____

_____

_____

Daily Notes

Let's Create

TODAY'S DATE:

DAILY GRATITUDE

★ ....

★ ....

★ ....

★ ....

★ ....

★ ....

TASKS FOR THE DAY

☐ ....

☐ ....

☐ ....

☐ ....

☐ ....

☐ ....

TODAY'S ACTION STEP TOWARDS MY GOAL

GOAL:

_____

_____

_____

_____

_____

Daily Notes

Let's Create

TODON'S DATE:

DAILY GRATITUDE

★ ....
★ ....
★ ....
★ ....
★ ....
★ ....

TASKS FOR THE DAY

☐ ....
☐ ....
☐ ....
☐ ....
☐ ....
☐ ....

TODAY'S ACTION STEP TOWARDS MY GOAL

GOAL:

_____

_____

_____

_____

_____

Daily Notes

Let's Create

TODAY'S DATE:

DAILY GRATITUDE

TASKS FOR THE DAY

★ .... ☐ ....

★ .... ☐ ....

★ .... ☐ ....

★ .... ☐ ....

★ .... ☐ ....

★ .... ☐ ....

TODAY'S ACTION STEP TOWARDS MY GOAL

GOAL:

_____

_____

_____

_____

_____

Daily Notes

Let's Create

TODAY'S DATE:

DAILY GRATITUDE

★ ....

★ ....

★ ....

★ ....

★ ....

★ ....

TASKS FOR THE DAY

☐ ....

☐ ....

☐ ....

☐ ....

☐ ....

☐ ....

TODAY'S ACTION STEP TOWARDS MY GOAL

GOAL:

Daily Notes

Let's Create

TODAY'S DATE:

DAILY GRATITUDE

TASKS FOR THE DAY

★ .... ☐ ....

★ .... ☐ ....

★ .... ☐ ....

★ .... ☐ ....

★ .... ☐ ....

★ .... ☐ ....

TODAY'S ACTION STEP TOWARDS MY GOAL

GOAL:

Daily Notes

Let's Create

TODAY'S DATE:

DAILY GRATITUDE

★ ....

★ ....

★ ....

★ ....

★ ....

★ ....

TASKS FOR THE DAY

☐ ....

☐ ....

☐ ....

☐ ....

☐ ....

☐ ....

TODAY'S ACTION STEP TOWARDS MY GOAL

GOAL:

_____

_____

_____

_____

_____

Daily Notes

Let's Create

TODAY'S DATE:

DAILY GRATITUDE   TASKS FOR THE DAY

★ ....   ☐ ....

★ ....   ☐ ....

★ ....   ☐ ....

★ ....   ☐ ....

★ ....   ☐ ....

★ ....   ☐ ....

TODAY'S ACTION STEP TOWARDS MY GOAL

GOAL:

Daily Notes

Let's Create

TODAY'S DATE:

DAILY GRATITUDE

★ ....

★ ....

★ ....

★ ....

★ ....

★ ....

TASKS FOR THE DAY

☐ ....

☐ ....

☐ ....

☐ ....

☐ ....

☐ ....

TODAY'S ACTION STEP TOWARDS MY GOAL

GOAL:

_____

_____

_____

_____

_____

Daily Notes

Let's Create

TODAY'S DATE:

DAILY GRATITUDE	TASKS FOR THE DAY

★ ....

☐ ....

★ ....

☐ ....

★ ....

☐ ....

★ ....

☐ ....

★ ....

☐ ....

★ ....

☐ ....

TODAY'S ACTION STEP TOWARDS MY GOAL

GOAL:

_____

_____

_____

_____

_____

Daily Notes

Let's Create

TODAY'S DATE:

DAILY GRATITUDE	TASKS FOR THE DAY
★	☐
★	☐
★	☐
★	☐
★	☐
★	☐

TODAY'S ACTION STEP TOWARDS MY GOAL

GOAL:

Daily Notes

Let's Create

TODAY'S DATE:

DAILY GRATITUDE	TASKS FOR THE DAY
★	☐
★	☐
★	☐
★	☐
★	☐
★	☐

TODAY'S ACTION STEP TOWARDS MY GOAL

GOAL:

Daily Notes

Let's Create

TODAY'S DATE:

DAILY GRATITUDE

★ ....

★ ....

★ ....

★ ....

★ ....

★ ....

TASKS FOR THE DAY

☐ ....

☐ ....

☐ ....

☐ ....

☐ ....

☐ ....

TODAY'S ACTION STEP TOWARDS MY GOAL

GOAL:

_____

_____

_____

_____

_____

Daily Notes

Let's Create

TODAY'S DATE:

DAILY GRATITUDE	TASKS FOR THE DAY

★ ....   ☐ ....

★ ....   ☐ ....

★ ....   ☐ ....

★ ....   ☐ ....

★ ....   ☐ ....

★ ....   ☐ ....

TODAY'S ACTION STEP TOWARDS MY GOAL

GOAL:

_____

_____

_____

_____

Daily Notes

Let's Create

TODAY'S DATE:

DAILY GRATITUDE	TASKS FOR THE DAY
★	☐
★	☐
★	☐
★	☐
★	☐
★	☐

TODAY'S ACTION STEP TOWARDS MY GOAL

GOAL:

Daily Notes

Let's Create

TODAY'S DATE:

DAILY GRATITUDE	TASKS FOR THE DAY
★	☐
★	☐
★	☐
★	☐
★	☐
★	☐

TODAY'S ACTION STEP TOWARDS MY GOAL

GOAL:

Daily Notes

Let's Create

TODAY'S DATE:

DAILY GRATITUDE	TASKS FOR THE DAY
★	☐ ....
★	☐ ....
★	☐ ....
★	☐ ....
★	☐ ....
★	☐ ....

TODAY'S ACTION STEP TOWARDS MY GOAL

GOAL:

Daily Notes

Let's Create

TODAY'S DATE:

DAILY GRATITUDE

TASKS FOR THE DAY

★ .... ☐ ....

★ .... ☐ ....

★ .... ☐ ....

★ .... ☐ ....

★ .... ☐ ....

★ .... ☐ ....

TODAY'S ACTION STEP TOWARDS MY GOAL

GOAL:

Daily Notes

Let's Create

TODAY'S DATE:

DAILY GRATITUDE

⭐ ....

⭐ ....

⭐ ....

⭐ ....

⭐ ....

⭐ ....

TASKS FOR THE DAY

☐

☐

☐

☐

☐

☐

TODAY'S ACTION STEP TOWARDS MY GOAL

GOAL:

Daily Notes

Let's Create

TODAY'S DATE:

DAILY GRATITUDE

TASKS FOR THE DAY

★ ....

☐ ....

★ ....

☐ ....

★ ....

☐ ....

★ ....

☐ ....

★ ....

☐ ....

★ ....

☐ ....

TODAY'S ACTION STEP TOWARDS MY GOAL

GOAL:

Daily Notes

Let's Create

TODODAY'S DATE:

DAILY GRATITUDE

★ ....

★ ....

★ ....

★ ....

★ ....

★ ....

TASKS FOR THE DAY

☐ ....

☐ ....

☐ ....

☐ ....

☐ ....

☐ ....

TODODAY'S ACTION STEP TOWARDS MY GOAL

GOAL:

Daily Notes

Let's Create

TODAY'S DATE:

DAILY GRATITUDE	TASKS FOR THE DAY
★	☐
★	☐
★	☐
★	☐
★	☐
★	☐

TODAY'S ACTION STEP TOWARDS MY GOAL

GOAL:

Daily Notes

Let's Create

TODAY'S DATE:

DAILY GRATITUDE

★ ....

★ ....

★ ....

★ ....

★ ....

★ ....

TASKS FOR THE DAY

☐ ....

☐ ....

☐ ....

☐ ....

☐ ....

☐ ....

TODAY'S ACTION STEP TOWARDS MY GOAL

GOAL:

_____

_____

_____

_____

Daily Notes

Let's Create

TODAY'S DATE:

DAILY GRATITUDE	TASKS FOR THE DAY
★	☐
★	☐
★	☐
★	☐
★	☐
★	☐

TODAY'S ACTION STEP TOWARDS MY GOAL

GOAL:

Daily Notes

Let's Create

TODODAY'S DATE:

DAILY GRATITUDE	TASKS FOR THE DAY
★	☐
★	☐
★	☐
★	☐
★	☐
★	☐

TODAY'S ACTION STEP TOWARDS MY GOAL

GOAL:

Daily Notes

Let's Create

TODAY'S DATE:

DAILY GRATITUDE

★ ....

★ ....

★ ....

★ ....

★ ....

★ ....

TASKS FOR THE DAY

☐ ....

☐ ....

☐ ....

☐ ....

☐ ....

☐ ....

TODAY'S ACTION STEP TOWARDS MY GOAL

GOAL:

_____

_____

_____

_____

_____

Daily Notes

Let's Create

TODAY'S DATE:

DAILY GRATITUDE

★ ....

★ ....

★ ....

★ ....

★ ....

★ ....

TASKS FOR THE DAY

☐ ....

☐ ....

☐ ....

☐ ....

☐ ....

☐ ....

TODAY'S ACTION STEP TOWARDS MY GOAL

GOAL:

_____

_____

_____

_____

_____

Daily Notes

Let's Create

TODAY'S DATE:

DAILY GRATITUDE	TASKS FOR THE DAY
★	☐ ....
★	☐ ....
★	☐ ....
★	☐ ....
★	☐ ....
★	☐ ....

TODAY'S ACTION STEP TOWARDS MY GOAL

GOAL:

Daily Notes

Let's Create

TODAY'S DATE:

DAILY GRATITUDE

★ ....

★ ....

★ ....

★ ....

★ ....

★ ....

TASKS FOR THE DAY

☐ ....

☐ ....

☐ ....

☐ ....

☐ ....

☐ ....

TODAY'S ACTION STEP TOWARDS MY GOAL

GOAL:

Daily Notes

Let's Create

TODAY'S DATE:

DAILY GRATITUDE	TASKS FOR THE DAY
★	☐
★	☐
★	☐
★	☐
★	☐
★	☐

TODAY'S ACTION STEP TOWARDS MY GOAL

GOAL:

Daily Notes

Let's Create

TODAY'S DATE:

DAILY GRATITUDE	TASKS FOR THE DAY

★ .... ☐ ....

★ .... ☐ ....

★ .... ☐ ....

★ .... ☐ ....

★ .... ☐ ....

★ .... ☐ ....

TODAY'S ACTION STEP TOWARDS MY GOAL

GOAL:

_____

_____

_____

_____

_____

Daily Notes

Let's Create

TODAY'S DATE:

DAILY GRATITUDE

★ ....

★ ....

★ ....

★ ....

★ ....

★ ....

TASKS FOR THE DAY

☐ ....

☐ ....

☐ ....

☐ ....

☐ ....

☐ ....

TODAY'S ACTION STEP TOWARDS MY GOAL

GOAL:

_____

_____

_____

_____

_____

Daily Notes

Let's Create

TODAY'S DATE:

DAILY GRATITUDE

TASKS FOR THE DAY

★ ....

☐ ....

★ ....

☐ ....

★ ....

☐ ....

★ ....

☐ ....

★ ....

☐ ....

★ ....

☐ ....

TODAY'S ACTION STEP TOWARDS MY GOAL

GOAL:

Daily Notes

7 steps to Creating my Goal

THE SIMPLE METHOD TO SUCCESS

1. The Goal I am creating:

_____

_____

2. I will achieve my goal by... (add a Date):

_____

3. The things I am doing to achieve my goal:

_____

_____

_____

_____

_____

_____

The best way to predict the future is to Create it....

- Abraham Lincoln

7 steps to Creating my Goal

THE SIMPLE METHOD TO SUCCESS

4. Organise the steps into a check list:

- [ ]
- [ ]
- [ ]
- [ ]
- [ ]
- [ ]
- [ ]
- [ ]
- [ ]

5. Set the Intention to **_Take action_** towards it.

6. **_Every day_** write the goal, write the action and take the action towards **The Goal**.

7. When you achieve it, go to the list of Goals and choose the next Goal in the same way as before.

If you follow this simple method you can achieve anything!

Nothing can stop you but yourself...

Hooked Living

Notes

ANYTHING ELSE YOU WOULD LIKE TO ADD

7 steps to Creating my Goal

THE SIMPLE METHOD TO SUCCESS

1. The Goal I am creating:

_____
_____

2. I will achieve my goal by... (add a Date):

_____

3. The things I am doing to achieve my goal:

_____
_____
_____
_____
_____
_____
_____

The best way to predict the future is to Create it....

- Abraham Lincoln

7 steps to Creating my Goal

THE SIMPLE METHOD TO SUCCESS

4. Organise the steps into a check list:

- [ ]
- [ ]
- [ ]
- [ ]
- [ ]
- [ ]
- [ ]
- [ ]
- [ ]

5. Set the Intention to **_Take action_** towards it.

6. **_Every day_** write the goal, write the action and take the action towards **_The Goal_**.

7. When you achieve it, go to the list of Goals and choose the next Goal in the same way as before.

If you follow this simple method you can achieve anything!

Nothing can stop you but yourself...

Hooked Living

Notes

ANYTHING ELSE YOU WOULD LIKE TO ADD

7 steps to Creating my Goal

1. The Goal I am creating:

_____

_____

2. I will achieve my goal by... (add a Date):

_____

3. The things I am doing to achieve my goal:

_____

_____

_____

_____

_____

_____

_____

_____

The best way to predict the future is to Create it....

– Abraham Lincoln

7 steps to Creating my Goal

THE SIMPLE METHOD TO SUCCESS

4. Organise the steps into a check list:

- [ ]
- [ ]
- [ ]
- [ ]
- [ ]
- [ ]
- [ ]
- [ ]
- [ ]

5. Set the Intention to **_Take action_** towards it.

6. **_Every day_** write the goal, write the action and take the action towards **_The Goal_**.

7. When you achieve it, go to the list of Goals and choose the next Goal in the same way as before.

If you follow this simple method you can achieve anything!

Nothing can stop you but yourself...

Hooked Living

Notes

ANYTHING ELSE YOU WOULD LIKE TO ADD

Printed in Great Britain
by Amazon